SPORTS
ALL-ST★RS

BRADLEY BEAL

Alexander Lowe

Lerner Publications ◆ Minneapolis

SPORTS THRILLS *MEET* RESEARCH SKILLS

Lerner SPORTS

Free Database Trial: **lernersports.com**

Lerner Publications Company
An imprint of Lerner Publishing Group, Inc.
241 First Avenue North
Minneapolis, MN 55401 USA

For reading levels and more information, look up this title at www.lernerbooks.com.

Main body text set in Albany Std. Typeface provided by Agfa.

Library of Congress Cataloging-in-Publication Data

Names: Lowe, Alexander, author.
Title: Bradley Beal / Alexander Lowe.
Description: Minneapolis : Lerner Publications, [2022] | Series: Sports all-stars | Includes bibliographical references and index. | Audience: Ages 7–11 | Audience: Grades 2–3 | Summary: "NBA shooting guard Bradley Beal's amazing offensive skills give the Washington Wizards a chance to win every game they play. Learn about his life, how he prepares for games, and what he does for fun"— Provided by publisher.
Identifiers: LCCN 2021030794 (print) | LCCN 2021030795 (ebook) | ISBN 9781728441160 (library binding) | ISBN 9781728445120 (ebook)
Subjects: LCSH: Beal, Bradley, 1993—-Juvenile literature. | Basketball players—United States—Biography—Juvenile literature. | Washington Wizards (Basketball team)—Juvenile literature.
Classification: LCC GV884.B43 L69 2022 (print) | LCC GV884.B43 (ebook) | DDC 796.323092 [B]—dc23

LC record available at https://lccn.loc.gov/2021030794
LC ebook record available at https://lccn.loc.gov/2021030795

Manufactured in the United States of America
1-49887-49730-7/15/2021

TABLE OF CONTENTS

SHOOTING STAR

Bradley Beal has been putting up points for the Washington Wizards since 2012.

Bradley Beal scored basket after basket for his team. He was determined to lead the Washington Wizards to victory against the Portland Trail Blazers. His teammates were struggling to pass him the ball when he was open for easy shots. So Beal had to create most of his shots himself. Impressive dribble moves and quick jump shots allowed him to build his scoring total. The 6 foot 3 (1.9 m) shooting guard was on fire.

FACTS
AT A GLANCE

- **Date of birth:**
  June 28, 1993

- **Position:** shooting guard

- **League:** National Basketball
  Association (NBA)

- **Professional highlights:**
  was the third overall pick in the
  2012 NBA Draft; once scored
  60 points in an NBA game; is a
  three-time NBA All-Star

- **Personal highlights:** grew up
  in St. Louis, Missouri; has four
  brothers who played college
  football; has two sons

Beal drives toward the basket against the Trail Blazers.

In the first half, Beal scored 19 points. The impressive total set him up well for one of the highest-scoring games in his career. His highest-scoring game had come the year before with 42 points against the Phoenix Suns.

As the fourth quarter began, the Wizards had a small lead. Beal needed to keep scoring to give his team a chance to win. He pulled up from deep behind the three-point line. The shot arced toward the basket and swished through the net. That gave him 43 points and a new career high. But there was still more work to do.

Beal kept scoring to help the Wizards pull away from the Trail Blazers. With 24 seconds left on the clock, he threw down a two-handed slam dunk. The score gave him 51 points in the game. The Wizards defeated the Trail Blazers 106–92.

After five years in the league, Beal had done it. He had his first 50-point game. He proved again that he was an NBA superstar.

Bradley averaged 32.5 points per game as a senior in high school.

Bradley Beal was born June 28, 1993, in St. Louis, Missouri. He is the middle child of Bobby and Besta Beal. Both of Bradley's parents were college

St. Louis (*pictured*) is the second biggest city in Missouri behind Kansas City.

athletes at Kentucky State University. Bobby played football and Besta played basketball. Bradley's mother taught him how to shoot a basketball when he was very young.

"She's been helping me out a lot," Bradley said. "Both my parents, my whole family, they're always behind me 100 percent. My mom, she's probably my biggest critic by far. That's what made me into the player I am today, just her pushing me and making me want to do better."

Bradley has four brothers. Bruce and Brandon are older than Bradley, and twins Byron and Bryon are younger. All four of Bradley's brothers are good athletes, and the competition in their backyard games helped make Bradley the player he is.

After a successful high school career at Chaminade College Preparatory School, Beal went on to play basketball at the University of Florida. Coach Billy Donovan had coached multiple players who

Beal lines up a shot during a high school game.

made it to the NBA, and he recruited Beal knowing he could be another star player. Beal played well in his first season and became a First-Team All-Southeastern Conference player. He was the conference Freshman of the Week six times during the 2011–2012 season.

Beal wears a Wizards hat and smiles at the 2012 NBA Draft.

After his freshman year, Beal decided to enter the 2012 NBA Draft. At the draft, NBA teams take turns choosing new players from colleges and other leagues around the world. Beal was one of the top players in the draft. The Wizards took him with the third overall pick. He had reached his dream of becoming an NBA player.

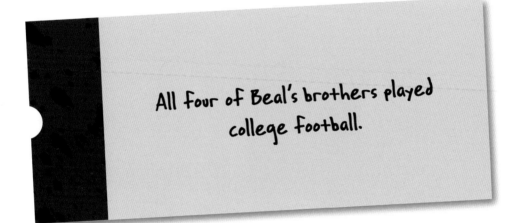

All four of Beal's brothers played college football.

Beal keeps the ball away from a defender in a game against the Chicago Bulls.

Since his 2012 NBA debut, Beal is among the league leaders in minutes played. This is something he has spent his whole career preparing for. Beal has made it his mission to be one of the best-trained players in the league. But sometimes, injuries strike.

Beal dunks the ball against the New York Knicks.

Beal had a stress reaction in his lower right leg in 2013. One of the bones there was overworked. If left untreated, a stress reaction can become a break. Beal took time off to recover, but luckily, the injury healed before the bone broke. Had it broken, he may have needed surgery. Beal has had minor

Beal celebrates after sinking a big shot.

issues with his leg since then, and he has had to miss a few games to recover.

Beal began working with shooting coach Drew Hanlen when Beal was only 13 years old. They still work together in the off-season to improve all aspects of Beal's game. "Ever since he's been a little kid," Hanlen said, "he's been a special, special worker. Him being in amazing shape is due to his tremendous work ethic."

Beal spends much of the season working on his shooting form.

Beal spends his off-season working on his fitness. He does high-intensity workouts to improve his cardio strength. He shoots without stopping for three minutes to get ready for the intense parts of NBA games. Beal also does obstacle courses that take 35 to 45 minutes to complete. Those sessions help his balance, strength, and speed.

Many NBA players post videos of their workouts on social media. But not Beal. He prefers to work out privately with no one watching. He wants everyone to see the results of his work on the court, not on social media.

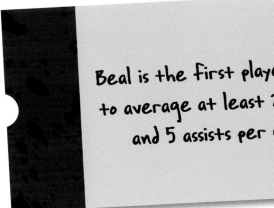

Beal is the first player in Wizards history to average at least 25 points, 5 rebounds, and 5 assists per game in a season.

A WIZARD OFF THE COURT

Wizards fans can't wait to see what Beal will do when he has the ball in his hands.

Beal wears Jordan Brand basketball shoes.

Beal's popularity as an NBA star has led to many business partnerships. He works with Jordan Brand. They provide his basketball shoes and other gear for games. He also has deals with Old Spice, Panini trading cards, Pepsi, and the Tissot watch company.

Nelly released his first album, *Country Grammar*, in 2000.

Beal is a husband and a father. He married his longtime partner Kamiah Adams in 2020. They have two sons named Bradley Jr. and Braylon.

The famous musician Nelly is a friend of the Beal family. When Beal was a child, Nelly would sometimes walk him to school. Nelly has praised Beal's strong family support, as well as his lifelong drive to achieve his dreams.

Beal worked with then-president Barack Obama in 2016 to raise awareness around an important social issue. Beal wants to help end gun violence in the United States. He even went to the White House to show his support.

Beal also helps people in the Washington, D.C., area. Since he moved there after being drafted by the Wizards, he has worked with the Wizards Care Charity. Through that program, Beal has provided school supplies, computers, and food to underserved communities in Washington, D.C.

Beal is a Baltimore Ravens fan. In 2019, he got to meet Ed Reed, a former Ravens player and one of his childhood heroes.

Beal accepts the 2018 NBA Cares Community
Assist award.

In 2018, Beal won the NBA Cares Community Assist
Award. It honors a player's commitment to positively
impacting his community over the course of the season.
The award is one of the highest honors in the NBA.

In 2019, Beal served as principal for a day at Ron Brown College Preparatory High School (RBHS). RBHS is an all-boys school in Washington, D.C. He held a private screening of the movie *Creed II* for RBHS students and other local community groups. He also gave each player and coach on the basketball team two pairs of shoes. Beal then took a group of students on a private tour of the National Museum of African American History and Culture.

The National Museum of African American History and Culture is part of Washington, D.C.'s, Smithsonian Institution.

Beal wants to be sure the young men at RBHS are set up for success in the future. He told them about the importance of graduating from high school. Later in 2019, Beal returned to RBHS and met with several students about their futures. Afterward, he took them bowling.

BEAL'S
FUTURE

Beal takes a shot during the 2014 NBA All-Star Game three-point contest.

Foot Locker

THREE-POINT
CONTEST

Beal has played in the NBA All-Star Game three times. He was first selected in the 2017–2018 season when he was 24 years old. If he keeps playing at his

In the 2021 season, the Wizards fought for a playoff spot, and every game mattered.

current level, he is likely to be selected for many more All-Star Games.

Beal scored 60 points against the Philadelphia 76ers on January 7, 2021. That equaled a team record that Gilbert Arenas achieved in 2006. Later that season, Beal had his fifth career 50-point game.

Beal (*right*) and Russell Westbrook (*left*) hope to lead the Wizards to many playoff wins.

For the past few seasons, trade rumors have surrounded Beal. He is the sort of young star who would make a great addition to some of the NBA's top teams. Despite Beal's play, the Wizards have not won many games in recent seasons. Some fans think he would be better off with a new team. But he said that he wants to stay in Washington. "It's tough because we want to win and I want to win," Beal said. "This is why I stayed, I want to win. I figure this is the place I can get it done."

The Wizards hope that with Beal, fellow star Russell Westbrook, and other good young players, they can win the Eastern Conference. Beal is a superstar who is ready to lead his team into the playoffs.

All-Star Stats

Bradley Beal is one of the best scorers in the **NBA**. Since his first season, he has consistently increased the points he has scored per game. The 2020–2021 season was one of his best. He ended up scoring the second-highest points per game of anyone in the league.

2020–2021 NBA Points Per Game Leaders

1.	Stephen Curry	32.0
2.	Bradley Beal	31.3
3.	Damian Lillard	28.8
4.	Joel Embiid	28.5
5.	Giannis Antetokounmpo	28.1
6.	Luka Doncic	27.7
7.	Zach LaVine	27.4
8.	Zion Williamson	27.0
9.	Kyrie Irving	26.9
10.	Jayson Tatum	26.4
10.	Donovan Mitchell	26.4
10.	Nikola Jokic	26.4

Glossary

cardio: relating to the heart and blood vessels

conference: a group of teams that play one another; the NBA has two conferences, the Eastern Conference and the Western Conference

debut: a first appearance

dribble: the act of moving a basketball forward by bouncing it

jump shot: a shot in basketball made by jumping into the air and releasing the ball with one or both hands at the peak of the jump

obstacle course: a training course filled with obstacles such as fences, walls, and ditches

off-season: when a sports league is inactive

recruit: to find new players and get them to join a team or other group

shooting guard: a guard in basketball whose chief role is as an outside shooter

slam dunk: a shot in basketball made by jumping high into the air and throwing the ball down through the basket

three-point line: a line on a basketball court beyond which a made basket counts for three points

Source Notes

9   "How Bradley Beal Broke Out," *SBNation*, February 27, 2013, https://www.sbnation.com /nba/2013/2/27/4035970/bradley-beal-washington -wizards-profile-rookie.

16   "How Bradley Beal Became Possibly the Best Conditioned Athlete in the NBA," *NBC Sports Washington*, March 7, 2019, https://www.nbcsports. com/washington/wizards/how-bradley-beal-became -possibly-best-conditioned-athlete-nba.

26 –27 Chase Hughes, "Bradley Beal on Whether He's Frustrated: 'Is the Sky Blue?,'" *NBC Sports Washington*, January 28, 2021, https://www.nbcsports .com/washington/wizards/bradley-beal-whether-hes -frustrated-losing-sky-blue.

Learn More

About Brad
http://bradleybeal.net/about/

Bradley Beal
https://www.nba.com/player/203078/bradley_beal

Community Assist Award
https://communityassist.nba.com/

Levit, Joe. *Basketball's G.O.A.T.: Michael Jordan, LeBron James, and More*. Minneapolis: Lerner Publications, 2020.

Monson, James. *Behind the Scenes Basketball*. Minneapolis: Lerner Publications, 2020.

Whiting, Jim. *Washington Wizards*. Mankato, MN: Creative Education, 2018.

Index

Photo Acknowledgments

Patrick Smith/Staff/Getty Images, p.4; Will Newton/Stringer/Getty Images, p.6; Chris Williams/Icon SMI 007/Newscom, p.8; Art Wager/Getty Images, p.9; Chris Williams/ Icon SMI 007/Newscom, p.10; Elsa/Staff/Getty Images, p.11; Rob Carr/Staff/Getty Images, p.13; Mark Goldman/Icon SMI 749/Newscom, p.14; Rob Carr/Staff/Getty Images, p.15; Patrick Smith/Staff/Getty Images, p.16; Rob Carr/Staff/Getty Images, p.18; Patrick Smith/Staff/Getty Images, p.19; Chris McKay/Stringer/Getty Images, p.20; Kevin Winter/Staff/Getty Images, p.22; Mark Wilson/Staff/Getty Images, p.23; Ronald Martinez/Staff/Getty Images, p.24; Tim Nwachukwu/Staff/Getty Images, p.25; Will Newton/Stringer/Getty Images, p.26

Cover: Patrick Smith/Staff/Getty Images